Heavenly Light, Celestial Bodies, & Us

Poems & Considerations

Audrey Yeardley

AuthorHouse™ UK Ltd.
500 Avebury Boulevard
Central Milton Keynes, MK9 2BE
www.authorhouse.co.uk
Phone: 08001974150

© *2010 Audrey Yeardley. All rights reserved.*

No part of this book may be reproduced, stored in a retrieval system, or transmitted by any means without the written permission of the author.

First published by AuthorHouse 2/9/2010

ISBN: 978-1-4490-3598-3 (sc)

This book is printed on acid-free paper.

Contents

The Moon was New	1
Aboriginal Dreams	2
I Observe The Snail	3
She is a fast traveller, Moon,	4
Proving Something	5
Miranda on the Move	6
Looking For Lambs in Whitehaven	7
Hecate Recalls Her Past Loves	8
We Fixed on You	10
When they Landed on You	11
Museum Piece	15
Moon, in All Her Glory	16
Scary Moon	17
Falling Out With The Moon	18
Look What the Wind Blew In	19
Orb Spinners	20
The Cello Player	21
Orbit	22
A Word in Your Shell-Like	23
The Odd Prawn	24
The Love Light in Your Eyes	25
Earth	26
My Friend and The Leaves	29
I Will Attempt Recompense, of a Kind.	30

Hi! Says Moon	31
Moon Said	32
Moon Just In, Is	33
I Dip My Finger	34
Moon's Manifesto	35
Story Musgrave	37
Now, Let's Talk About Pluto	38
Monday is Moon Day	39
Was Meant to Be, but Not Like This	40
Old Moon Keeps on Making Her Mind Up	43
The Women Who Have Lost Their Voices	44
One More Heavenly Light	45
When Peter Skellern Sings, He Makes me Cry	46
Moon's Feeling Feisty	47
Moon Says	48
Oh, Happy Moon	49
Actually, says Moon	50
Things Change	51
You mustn't Fuck a Fairy (A sad tale)	52
Fish Wives	53
A Postcard	54
About the Author	59

For seven years I lived a close to the Moon as I could get. It was the 1960's and, for me, a kind of paradise. It had been my idea to go to live at a remote Inn, high above sea level, and life was never going to be easy, but those years brought me much joy.
It wasn't so very far from where Wordsworth had written:

> "Bliss was it in that dawn to be alive,
> But to be young was very heaven! -Oh times,
> In which the meagre, stale, forbidding ways
> Of custom, law and statute, took at once
> The attraction of a country in romance."

I have, always, aspired to live in "country" places, where I can most feel the enchantment of the Universe, and the changing seasons but here, on the wild moors, where the only sounds in the night were the calls of Pewits, was my own "very heaven."

Sometimes, when the Moon was bathing the landscape with its silver light, I would get out of my bed to stand outside, listening to the star music; falling into its enchantment and knowing that (no matter what was happening down here, on Earth, all was right in that greater Elsewhere).

Every so often I feel impelled to go back to recapture that bliss, and the inner freedom; and it never fails. It isn't just "going back" but more like "being back."
And, of course, there was the amazingly charged energy of the music of the Sixties that seemed, for a time, as though it might change this tired old world.

From time to time, a group of officers would come over the A66, from Catterick, to spend the night with us. One of them was Jim, a lovely man with an interest in the prospect of space travel, and in UFO's.
He used to say that these high moors were where, if he was an alien, he would choose to land his spacecraft.
Fast forward to July 20th, in 1969, when over 500 million people,

worldwide, watched Neil Armstrong stepped on to the surface of the Moon, I thought of Jim.
No longer where my spirit felt so much at home, I watched from the garden of the small house we had moved to, praying that we wouldn't make a mess of things, now we had the power to travel through the Universe.
That "one small step for a man" was the precursor for giant leaps, if only we can live up to all of the potential that we have, within our DNA, to become fully qualified human beings.

When those first, and utterly beautiful, impressions of Earth, as seen from the Moon were beamed to Us, should have been a very big Wake-Up Call. The fact that, for so many of Us, it wasn't is a tragedy.

Earth and Moon are so closely entwined and made of such similar materials means they can be thought of as being Celestial Sisters. As Earth's satellite, there is overwhelming evidence that Moon came about as the result of a very significant impact. In cosmic terms, a Universal Event that created a unique relationship.

Since Time Immemorial Mankind has looked to the skies for signs, portents and answers.
And, being a story-telling species, created a host of myths and legends.
It wasn't long before astronomy and astrology became a part of our attempts to understand the environment we lived in; what lay beneath and what was above.
The priests of both ancient Babylonia and the Hellenistic Greeks were to establish what has become an abiding fascination for every succeeding century and in which Sun and Moon ranked as being the most important influences.

Long recognised as representing the feminine side of a Woman's nature, reflecting the light from the Sun, Moon also encompasses an internalised response to what happens in our personal domain.
And, because Moon changes her astrological sign approximate-

ly every two and a half days, so She exerts an influence on our moods, and responses.

It has been said, and it has the ring of a truth, that every one of Us is a planet, with our own Sun, Moon and Stars. Each one of us travels in orbit with others, following a personal destiny.
The position of both Sun and Moon in our natal charts, are the prime movers, pre-programming our responses to what cards Fate has dealt us.

The Sun represents your father, and how you will respond to masculine influences in your life. He encourages you to begin the journey of self-knowledge, to create your own public image; to stand up for your Self.

The Moon represents your mother and, because She rules the deeply mysterious and, for the most part, unconscious levels of past life memories Her drive will be towards finding emotional security.

Sometimes Sun and Moon, in appearing to have different and, quite often, different agendas find themselves in conflict and yet, each have a need for each other.
Sometimes that's enough to drive some of Us quite crazy.

The Universe, as well as being All That It Is, is a mass of hidden messages. Quantum Physics is beginning to unravel some of them but, let's all hope that it will be on a Need to Know basis. Mankind has a way of getting above itself- as anyone with memories of Atlantis will understand.
The Ancient Mystery Schools had some brief but pertinent words written above their porticos: "Know Thyself."
Once we do, we're on the road to enlightenment, when Sun and Moon work in harmony.
When they do is when each does what it does best. Moon listens, considers, searches through the files of her intuition and nourishes the radiant Sun, in all his glory.
Happy Woman/Happy Man.

In the best of all possible worlds, that's what makes the perfect Man/Woman relationship.
Never give up, for it's Love that makes the world go round.

Begin your own exploration by seeking out an Astrologer, so that you can make a study of your individual natal chart to see how Sun and Moon are functioning in the blueprint; and, then, to your own Self, be true.
We are all Work in Progress.

The relationship of our parents is "written in our stars."
In my "story" I had to learn (often in a hard way) to let go of any outgrown attachments to both friends and lovers.
I inherited a complexity of knots from my mother, and her maternal lineage that, in bedevilling me for the most of my life, has led to a greater understanding of what drives me.
Saturn's placement has a lot to do with this. He rarely lets you off the hook, keeping you to dutiful engagements.

And Pluto! Ah, Pluto! Whenever he makes his presence felt is when everything changes.
Pluto is no dwarf, whatever some might say. He is an all-or-nothing planet, and takes no hostages. A Transit of Pluto can feel like the most searching colonic irrigation, ever.

Just consider the company that inhabits the Universe, and how they influence us.
There's Mercury, Venus, Mars, Jupiter, Uranus, Neptune; all of these planets exert an influence on our daily doings, and our ultimate plan.

Deeper within are the complex workings of the asteroids, Chiron, Ceres, Pallas, Juno and Vesta, significant parts of this fascinating array of cosmic mechanics.
All of these work in unison, but the most obvious players in our lives are Sun and Moon.

There's more to Astrology than meets the eye.

Your natal is a symbolic map of your consciousness, and a tool to help you navigate your way though "bad" times and "good" times.

We may have forgotten, and we may have become waylaid by other's agendas, but every one of Us on Planet Earth has come for a reason.

Whatever we choose to experience is a seed. Nothing is ever wasted but it's a long journey to understanding who we really are.

The Moon was New

The Moon was New, when I was born,
A fact that pleased us.
None of that waning,
Nor waxing full, that drives some mad.
New: not second hand: freshly introduced
And unfamiliar.
Unaccustomed.
You'd have thought we'd got it made.
Hah!
World says: "Stuff that, Matey. You'll do what we do.
What's been done, before. What's good enough for us is good enough for you.
Why change the habits of lifetimes?"

That was the first hit.

Aboriginal Dreams

My mother should have been a Movie Star;
Instead, she travelled to Australia
Where Her Man Did Her Wrong.
Very, Very Wrong.
It is night time; and the men are cloaked in their kangaroo skins,
Floating on paper bark rafts, seeking crocodiles.
They're alert for bubbles,
And their silent laughter.
Crocodiles.
So it was with my mother;
Crocodiles in her life, endlessly.
Crocodiles haunting my dreams,
Aboriginals, my kith and kin.
On, and on, and on.
My mother should have been a Movie Star.

I Observe The Snail

It is the Night of the New Moon,
And the Gypsy Woman has come to our door.
This year, my Mother will not buy her lace,
Nor her flowers;
Nor hear what fortune will befall her.
"Rubbish," she says. "It's all rubbish."
Caught in my miserable whooping
(All the children, all around are whooping)
And a War on,
I yearn to know.
She has the look of a Spell Weaver, A Healer, a Seer;
All the things I need from a Mother.
And so, I listen.
I observe the snail:
Tecciztecatl is in its shell,
And the snail linked to the moon.
Gathered from my father's garden,
It trails through sugar: through silver slime.
Everything has a significance, now.
From deep in my underworld, and snared,
I observe the Snail, my Mother,
And the Gypsy Woman,
Knowing, this time, I am on familiar territory.
This time I will come back, unharmed.
I drink the juice.

She is a fast traveller, Moon,

Skimming through the Signs,
Making portents.
Babylonians made Her Male.
One of their rare errors of judgement.
More is expected of Woman, than Man.
Romans made their lustrum ceremonials,
Purifying their entire complement of blame,
Every five years, after a census,
A full-sweeping under the carpet confessional.
No wonder she threatened the Momentous and the Calamitous.
I do much the same.
You shouldn't mess with Moon.
Take note as you go about your domestic business,
Of the Peony; waxing as She waxes,
Waning, as She wanes.
In Her undertow is Knowing.

Proving Something

To prove I was not on the right road,
I travelled the wrong road, wilfully;
Knowing it was wrong; just to see where it took me.
Knowing I would go to the proof of knowing
I was on the wrong road.
There are many roads to Right or Wrong.
Sometimes, the wrong road takes us right.
And even the right road can lead us awry,
Unless we know the difference.
And, sometimes, we are led to the wrong road
To simply give a direction to someone who is lost

Miranda on the Move

When the marriage broke up, within the week,
And seven days and night of pique,
Miranda rose, and put her finger on the map.
She packed her bags and went to Shap
(Which used to be in Westmorland
But it was early closing day so,
She stumbled to St. Bees)
It seemed to be The Hand of Fate,
Although she was in sorry state.
But, finding naught, she hurried on,
Until she came to Ulverston.
"I spit on Rue," Miranda cried. "I need some fun."
So that was that, and it was done.
For all I know, she's travelling still.
I hope she did. I hope she will.

Looking For Lambs in Whitehaven

Suffice it to say, everything was coincidental,
As I found my way to Whitehaven.
I slept, that night, close to the lambing field.
They were coming in twos, and threes,
And the frost settling.
I woke to the calls, and went, searching.
They sprang, muddled by our voices..
Me, stumbling, lending a hand,
And looking up at the stars, marvelling.
Tier upon tier of silver and shimmer,
Above and below.
The sounds of the sea, shifting beneath the cliffs.
The whole universe was singing.
Breathing and bleating, mingling.
Making magic of a place, so grey by morning.

Hecate Recalls Her Past Loves

Oh yes.
She has loved.
And, in her waning, weeps for its passing.
She writes by the light of torches, makes sigils of their names,
Tracks them through the signs,
Keeps a well of bitter brews.
She dwells in a very dark place,
Singing to the serpents in her hair,
Marvelling at the sloughing of skins.
She keeps no mirrors here.
Twelve times a year she does it,
This nine days of wailing
And no respite.
I watch her disappear, holding my breath, and ears
Against the sounds of her passing.
Oh yes, I have looked in my mirror, also.
I have looked to my chart, in despair.
Water, Fire, Earth and Air,
I note the journey of the Goddesses in my own cycle.
Mnemosyne, in The Waters

This is where she lies,
Which is where she has to be, lying in the water;
And listening,
Waiting for the turbulent voices.
Some way off, her maidens are waiting,
Dreading the wailing.
Some will stop their ears.

The ones who suffered most, will be the first.
It is their right; and it is the first net

(made of her own hair)
That will hold them.
These are memories made in shadows,
And their stories so terrible that some will stop their ears.
Mnemosyne listens to them all; it is their right.
These are the ones that come in the night, now,
Not to frighten the children.
Even though, some way off, some have already awoken,
Dreading the wailing; stopping their ears.

This is the First Welling; and Mnemosyne weeps.
Soon the nets will be full to their brimming,
And her maidens will come, with their singing.

Not for the first time, Mnemosyne wonders,
At past terribleness, and present terrors;
And the different mutations of awfulness
Lying in wait, for man's inhumanity to man.
Soon, she thinks, even the River will be full to its brimming.
This is where the Priests will be struck dumb.
As each year passes, she thinks, it comes closer.

We Fixed on You

We fixed on you, my Moon and I,
Desiring beyond Our reach.
And should not have; not in a month of Sundays.
Shame on us that we did.
Except, it was a collusion.
On the other hand your Moon, and you, did much the same.
Who's to blame?
Fuck the Fates who wove the threads,
Pulled us close, then cut us dead.
Oh yes.
Moon has a Dark Side, which you hid.
Bastard.
Your mother did for you.
So, crabwise, you struck me.

When they Landed on You

I never thought I'd come to the day
When they'd land on you.
It was a tour de force,
A slap in your face,
This rather stupid space race,
All Hoorah Henry's, Mouths and Big Baggy Trousers.
I hope you laughed, after the shock of it.
I always laugh after the shock of anything,
That it could have caught us so unawares, mostly.
After all was said and done, between us,
We were beginning to
Understand the Ways of Man.
Well, I thought we were,
But, than again, I guess you had the last laugh
When that bastard, with his Moon in Cancer,
Flattened me.
Christ. It hurts.

There are, as most women know, three stages in her life, all guided by the Triple Goddess: Maiden, Mother, Crone.
Each has its own, inherent, inherent beauty but coming into Crone can be the most blessed of all.

Some astrologers believe that while the Sun represents one's relationship to the divine Spirit, and our Ascendant having its bearing on our physical body, it is Moon who is the direct link to Soul.
She is the Keeper of Memory, of our deepest secrets; and the vessel we sail in, to explore our emotions.

Dwelling some two hundred and twenty five, seven hundred and forty five miles from Sister Earth, Moon stays in each of the twelve astrological signs for approximately two and a half days, on her journey from New to Full.
From that distance, she exerts a powerful and responsive fluctuation in the seas and tides; and in feelings.
In Tarot, Moon rules the sign of Cancer but she has more than a superficial influence on the two other watery signs of Scorpio and Pisces.

Many poems have been written about Moon. Walter de la Mare wrote one of the most beautiful, recently voted as 80th out of 500 Top Poems:

> "Slowly, silently, now the Moon,
> Walks the night in her silver shoon.
> This way, and that, she peers and sees
> Silver fruit and silver trees."

Most probably, it was first heard in Primary School, read by a teacher who had loved it, in her childhood.
Most certainly it brings home the magic and the mystery of this beautiful Orb.

It was Miss Clarke, my first teacher (and a kind of substitute mother figure) who instilled a love of nature in me. I owe her much,

particularly for instilling in me a love of words; of literature and myth.
She was to teach, well into her Seventies, and there should be more like her. Except, she might well have been married had it not been for the Great War, which killed so many men and prospective husbands.

Like many other children, growing up in a Time of War, we got used to the Black-Out, keeping lights to a minimum so that enemy aircraft would be able to spot any targets.
With both car and bicycle lights being "half-hooded," and the use of torches curbed, we learned to make the most of the natural light of Moon and Stars.

As the industrial world has spread, so comes an increasing light pollution which threatens to hid that light. I think we lose that living correspondence between Earth and The Heavens, to our severe detriment.

One of my early, and happier, memories of my mother was of her passing down something she had learned from my grandmother. When the Moon is New (and, it's considered unlucky to see it, firstly, through a window) you should go into the garden with a silver coin in your hand.

Then, as you look at the faint outline high in the sky, turn the coin three times in the palm of your hand, as you chant: "Your Servant, Dear Moon."
Now is the time to Make your Wish.
Nowadays I've gone one further, having a Wish Tree in my garden. My Inner Child just loves the pretty colours, and the movement among the branches.

On the night of New Moon I seek out a piece of coloured paper, about the size of a playing card, and write three wishes in my best handwriting before rolling it up (like a cigarette) and wrapping it round with a pretty ribbon.

Then, I hang it on my Wish Tree.

With the New Moon comes a wonderful opportunity for "new beginnings."
This is a time when the Sun and Moon are conjunct, so we can never be too sure how the energies will "marry up."
This is a time to make the plans, and to keep the options open.

When Moon is in her waxing phase (lasting for about nine and a half days) She brings a time when everything is absorbed more easily. It's a time to be Out and About, and to revise your plans. She looks to the Future, as All of Us really should.

Full Moon has a very special feel about it. If you are a very sensitive soul, you'll find yourself having a few sleepless nights, as She approaches this stage. It's highly likely that your dreams and inspirations will be running at full tilt; as will your emotions.
Be creative; listen to music; take note of all that is beautiful around you.

When Moon comes into Her Waning Time you may well feel like going deeper into your Self, needing time on your own. It's a time for shedding things that no longer work.

And, if you're a budding gardener, don't forget that planting and harvesting by the Moon's influence will bring you more chances for success.

Museum Piece

I saw a terracotta once; of women kneading dough.
Moving in time to a flute player's tune:
And I wondered at what we have lost.
That small scenario was fashioned,
When daily doings had a certain style,
And there was joy in domestic things.
You only had to look at their drinking cups to know
They weren't dull.
That little life had breath in it, still:
A fragment on which I mused.
What will last of us;
And just what is it that kept that brave place alive,
In every speck of dust?

Moon, in All Her Glory

"Well, They're doing us all proud tonight,"
Says the Old Lady,
Knitting long scarves on her wooden-slat porch.
(A stitch in time having saved the lives of nine goddesses.)
She sucks on her silver cigarette holder, given as a gift.
It bears simple words of gratitude:
"Do what you can.
with what you have,
with where you are."
It is a long cigarette holder.
She has had a long life.
The goddesses have long memories.
She did a very good thing.

Scary Moon

Oh, She's scary when She goes,
Seeking Reparations for old Wounds,
Hand in hand with Karma.
When She goes looking, there's no hiding.
When she chooses, you'll be hag-ridden.
Know this.
If you ever betrayed Her with a kiss,
Or, did Dirty Work,
She'll find you, when least expected.
Your kind,
Sneaky,
Will pay the Dues,
When She knocks at your door.
She knows when you're in,
Having looked through every window.
Oh yes. She's Scary

Falling Out With The Moon

Molly's fallen out with the Moon.
Not sure that it's temporary.
Probably not,
Given that It's come over,
Implacable.
She has become implacable.
In the night, Molly wakens,
Knowing It's coming full,
Will soon shine through her window,
Not even attempting a conversation,
Being silent, and remote,
Being implacable.
Molly casts a cold eye on the Moon,
And resolves this is, most certainly,
Not temporary.

Look What the Wind Blew In

Wanting tit for tat, and natural justice,
Her hand went to the tree.
Being a Rowan, It listened.
More than that, so had Moon.
A dark night, and a terrible wind gusting.
Christ!
They were terrible things he had said.
Moon had cried out: "Curse him! Go for it, Girl."
So, she had.
Moon cursed him.
In Inverness, a man cried out.
"Tough!" says Moon.
"That was just for Starters!"
This is my terrible night; dark, and the wind's gusting.
Moon's in a Bad Place.

Orb Spinners

This life we make
(a heart strung thing)
Starts with a bridge thread;
Is warp and weft,
Deft through our fingers.
Our quickening, led by a distant pulse,
And our web's woven with keen precision.
We are orb spinners.
Round and around these lines
(crossing and being crossed)
We spin the stories,
Testing their strengths,
Refashioning irregularities.
Listen to the spindles sing.
Do not unpick me.

The Cello Player

He played for us. Remember this.
He played for us, and it was not enough.
This is the sadness.
There were stars out that night,
And all was ripe for loving.
I was always ripe for loving.
Remember this, as you kiss your ordinary woman.
He did not play for you.
He played for us,
And every note hung on cold air,
And every note begged you to love me,
And every note wept for your blind intransigence,
For your refusal of something laid upon an altar.

Orbit

I spy with my little eye, Me,
In the sea.
Something beginning with M.
Magnificent Moon,
My celestial body makes poets swoon,
Dogs howl, and women weep.
Do not dare to speak of borrowed light;
That I do not shine by my own.
No man can look at Sun, for long,
Except go blind from gold.
I am kinder, more silver.
I am fields of forces you do not fully understand.
In Scorpio I seek the roots of things bringing you grief.
Thieves cannot hide from my sight,
Nor betrayers.
I have risen from my deep.
Spell me: "Help me all my powers to keep."
I am Magnificent and Beneficent Moon.
Do not cross me.

A Word in Your Shell-Like

"A word in your ear," says Moon.
She's lying on a beach; and it's not Troon,
Somewhere quite exotic.
She travelled there by Air, of course.
How else? It's Her Domain.
And no queuing.
She's on holiday: is New, ready for a Fling,
Casting off all Her cares.
"World can take a hike," she's thinking.
All around is Music; the sounds of guitars.
Sun's burning on the sand.
She smiles, takes out Factor Trillions Plus,
And, oh so gently, holds His hand.

The Odd Prawn

The Odd Prawn avoided his own kind,
Preferring the company of Whelks,
Limpets, Mussels, and Crabs:
Anyone, who wasn't Prawnish.
(They said he took after his mother.
Stuck Up.)
She lived on a floating island, made of fronds,
Drank champagne.
Lights on, all night.
(You could only guess what she got up to.)
His own kind (Prawnish) said he was Decidedly Queer.
But, the company he kept
(Mostly in beer)
Thought he was Delightfully Different; if a bit inept.
Strange things: words.
Being eccentric; being funny. It's all in the brain,
Except: the one is cherished:
The other, thought insane.

The Love Light in Your Eyes

The love light in your eyes
was never, ever there.
Beware, said my heart.
Beware.
But, nevertheless, I fell.
Falling like a fool, out of the tower,
out of my rut,
out of my power.
And, more is the pity,
out of my mind.
Hindsight is unkind,
when Love is blind.
The love light in your eyes
Was never, ever, there.
It was my reflection that I saw.

Earth

Here is The Place where We Tell Stories.
And Do The Time.
All of them are Elements of Us,
Exploring: Being a Hero;
Being the Ones Who Did the Crime:
Practising Blame.
Christ! What a Mess We Make of It,
In Your Name.
Six Days You took, preparing The Ground,
And on The Day You rested, I guess we ran loose.
Cain was closest to the Fall; the first to kill.
Eve couldn't handle him; nor what came after.
All that slaying.
Disaster, after disaster, after disaster.
And then, The Holocaust.
Whoever thought up Burnt Offerings,
Slaughtered animals on Your Altar,
Cursed us all with Ideological Contradictions.

At least, with animals, we know their markings: that they will sting, bite, mark our smell for miles and then spring, have their season for mating; and their long treks to the feeding grounds.

Like Whitman: I think, sometimes, I will go and live with the animals, and eat more human beings.

If we had the eyes to see all of Us, in all of our glory, as spiritual creatures in an evolving Universe -all at the same Time- then we'd truly know the meaning of Awe.
Instead most of Us grub around in mundane matters, not seeing the wonders that are waiting to be recognised.

Pascal said:
"Earthly things must be known, to be loved. Divine things must be loved, to be known."

Scientific Facts:

In shining by reflected light, Moon radiates a silvery hue. Silver is a mirror-creating element. As a metal it is the best known reflector of light, and has the highest electrical and thermal conductivity.

Most of the World's Silver is found, dissolved in Earth's Oceans.

Silver is used by the Movie Makers to create images on "The Silver Screen."

It is no accident that Moon rules Imagination and Fantasy; Dreams and Shadows.
In changing It's astrological signature, approximately every two and a half days Woman is able to experience the gamut of emotions expressed in the Cycle of the Moon.

Do this for Your Self: seek out a Journal and, for a whole Month, get in touch with your changing moods.
It will open your eyes.
What's more, you will never again, be able to ignore Her power.

We live on a Planet, where Karma waxes and wanes. Earth is a place where We all reap what we have sown; and where we can make dreams come true.

Everything is a matter of Timing.
Life doesn't have to be a Nightmare, nor ruled by Lunacy.

But, first, we have to remember, in being "Such Stuff as Dreams are Made On," some of us have come to shift some of the Bad Stuff.
And do what Mark Twain once said: "Dream other Dreams, and better."

My Friend and The Leaves

My friend does not sweep up leaves.
She leaves them on her lawn so that priest and neighbour
Would have her down; as a Sinner.
Only occasionally does she pick the brambles,
And only when there's a proper reason.
My friend will not be pushed.
Therefore my friend is at odds with the world she lives in.
Except it is not their world that she lives in.
Their world is a very small world,
Turning on a few degrees.
Where the leaves are gathered in droves, and burned.
They look at her leaves, talking among themselves
And, probably, would tell the priest,
Except he is long gone.
When word gets to her, that they are talking, among themselves,
She tells the messenger:
"I am waiting for the big wind. It always comes."

I Will Attempt Recompense, of a Kind.

I will attempt to make a poem out of a betrayal of the heart.
I know the moment when it began,
When I betrayed my own.
A poet has come to town,
And I am reminded.
This is the poet who digs deep for truth,
Tills the ground where others have made a quick harvest,
Is not content with platitudes.
I love this poet for not liking platitudes.
His words sprang off the page,
When I read them, causing my heart to stop its chattering.
Now, his voice is like a murmuring of bees
Or waves, upon a distant shore,
Comforting my blood.
I wept blood, when I betrayed myself,
When I allowed you to betray me,
When I became less than authentic.
I'd Like to Run This Past You

Hi! Says Moon

"Hi," says Moon,
"Sorry about the din.
We tried to drop lightly, but the tide wasn't in."

She laughs,
"Metaphorically speaking,
Having hung over your head
Since, Oh, since you were so high."
She's holding a vessel in Her hands.
It's made of silver.

"We'd like to run this past you, as your triplet Sister,.
Sometimes we act as One.
And I sure am, now, Bitch.
Disconcerting, coming from the same womb.
That you'd do what you've done,
Shagged the Sun.
But then Earth was made a whore by so many.

(She sighs)

Strange, when We who shape your moods and cycles aren't fecund.
That's our bane, and our curse; that we can't make children.
Sun has spoken. Says: Between Our waxing, and Our waning,
Our turning
Seemingly We are distant.
Not so.
We came to disavow you, and Him.
We are passionate.
Be very sure of that.
We are affronted.
(The vessel twangs: echoes with the sounds of women weeping.)
Come see the empty sky."

Moon Said

Moon said: I'm quite pissed off with your mendacity,
You've been spreading rumours, again.
Earth glances, surreptitiously at her guests,
Says, with her hand on the receiver:
"That's a travesty of the truth, sister."
This is not the time, nor the place.
You're waxing again, and things get exaggerated
When you're in one of your moods.
Moods? Me? Says Moon, viciously,
There's reasons in plenty.
Don't get me started.
I can see you all enjoying yourselves,
At my expense.
What happened to my inheritance?
Earth said: I'll speak with you,
When You're in Libra.
She draws the curtains, and takes a deep sip
From her wine cup.

Moon Just In, Is

Oh yes, She Is,
In All Her Glory.
There's no dearth of Splendour,
Nor Atmospheres, emanating from Craters.
She thrives on capital letters.
Not letting on much about her Dark Side,
And Mysterious Moods.
In her wardrobes, twelve gowns,
Spick and span and freshly laundered,
Not easy, when you have no water,
But she has her ways,
Always ready for Journeys.
Never, in a month of Moon Days, missing her Call.
Never fluffing her lines, and Up There, like the Trooper She is.
Up, where She belongs.
Moon, just in, Is
September's when She's at her Best,
So, Light a Candle
For the Harvest.

I Dip My Finger

I dip my finger in and, having tasted, draw back.
I do not like the taste of grief.
Some things are best left, imagined, I'm thinking.
Still, one has to keep on testing.
I try again, watching the ripples settle.
You are not here.
And the house is bare.
I cease playing games.

Moon's Manifesto

"Manifest your Dreams," sings Moon,
Speaking to the Women,
All decked out in Her Glory,
Resplendent in one of twelve gowns,
She's personally designed for this Grand Tour of The Heavens.
Behind, the orchestra,
Led by a smiling Apollo (a cheesy smile)
Playing razzle-dazzle tunes.

"One Year, and One Year Only,
By Cosmic Demand,
The Myths Revealed."

In Her first personal interview, syndicated across continents,
Moon has revealed some of the personal secrets that have made
Her what She is, today.

A Tough Life:
Born in a rough neighbourhood, raped by Her father, abandoned
by Her mother, and a Child removed from Her custody,
There were Times when She when she contemplated ending it,
All of It.

" I looked into the Void, "She says,
"And what saved me,
Was The Distant Songs of Women;
Which is the name for my latest album.
I listened to them, in the night.
And, they saved me, the voices of the countless women,
The unknown women, who had faith in me,
That I would put things right."

She sings: " It's quite a story, and it's your story,
Our Manifesto,
And they're your words and mine,
Of men who've used us, and things that changed us,
And still we find the strength to keep on going,
In spite of all the pain."

She smiles: "A myth of our own making, really."

Story Musgrave
Never Got to The Moon

Story never got to The Moon; not to stand on, anyway.
But Hey! Who cares?
He heard The Music.
He heard The Music; went Mystical.
Fifty Seven Octaves below the Middle,
Is The Music.
Beat that for a game of soldiers.

I think we'll stay Fucked,
Until we're all Singing the Same Tune.

Now, Let's Talk About Pluto

Because, when he turns up, everything goes pear-shaped.
This is what Pluto does, Big Time.
Makes you a small, cold and distant world.
And nothing is the same, ever again.
Ever, Ever, Ever.
When they made him Dwarf, I laughed.
Except, it was a hollow laugh.
Like you were, a hollow man
(a real dwarf)
Like everything was made hollow, eaten by maggots.
Like my heart was.
Ravaged.
Empty.
Dead.
Just look at the craters.
I hadn't bargained on you making such a mess of everything.
Hah!
Just Goes to Show.
But, actually, though I'm a lot less nice, for your coming,
(A lot less Nice)
Am more streetwise;
Should thank you for that.
You're a pal.
I had you, way out of my orbit,
(all touched by silver; all an illusion
Missing those crabs; and their scuttling.
Missing the damage they did, with their pincers)
Why do you think Moon became really scary?
Why do you think She hides her Dark Side.
And, once in Her While, spends her nights weeping?
It's one big wound, babe.
Still.

Monday is Moon Day

My day, says Moon, rising from Her bed, as Sun sets
She has dreamed Him, and is fulfilled.
He has dreamed her, and has willed a certain satisfaction.
She has allowed it.
My day for spells and scrying, says Moon,
Supping her latte.
She is Full.

Sitting in Starbucks, dwelling on Personal Issues,
The woman considers her position.
She mouths the words:
"Lady of Dreams be my inspiration;
Gypsy of the Skies be my guide;
Queen of the Night be my protector."
It is Done

Was Meant to Be, but Not Like This

It was meant to be simple.
Well, to put it another way: I thought it would be simple.
Easy peasy, really: in The Bag.
Hah!
What did I know?
They, always, bring in The Unexpected,
Even though They promise the Earth.
Not meant to be easy; not meant to be a walkover;
Not meant to be predictable,
Even though They've worked on the Charts,
And plotted the planetary courses.
I'd put them to the back of my mind, kind of.
I'd engaged in rather too much optimism.
I'd, also, bitten off more than I could chew.
So, I was ripe for a Fall.
Hah!
I'd forgotten about the Asteroids, and The Dwarves.

We live on a Planet, the only one that allows us Choices, where we come to reap what we have sown.
Everyone of Us has the power to make a Dream, or a Nightmare.
Everything is a matter of timing.
We have a word for this: Karma.

What goes around, comes around. Once we really come to terms with this concept, then we truly begin to understand the language, and the lessons of, Compassion.
Forgiveness (always a tricky issue for us Humans) becomes so much easier when we understand that every one of Us has to live with the consequences of their actions.
In due time, when we have walked in the shoes of those we have mistreated, comes an adjustment of our behaviours to our fellow beings.
That's you, me and Us.

Every Culture has it's own Mythologies, all based on their "takes" on the Universe.
Gods and Goddesses, as archetypes of human behaviour, enact the going to both Love and to War in their domains and dynasties; perceive "friends" and "enemies," defend their territorial rights, and mimic our dilemmas, here on Earth.
It's so much easier to study the "dysfunctional" when it's far removed.

Closer to home, it's more difficult not to become embroiled.
Every one of Us carries within, both warring and loving archetypes. The winner is, as the Elders know, the one we have fed the most.

Those who study the Tarot know that each card represents either an Archetype or a possibility in which to engage.
C.J. Jung, as one who did, pondered long on the Lovers Card, seeing as a representation of the Anima and the Animus, being the innermost part of the personality, or Soul.

When we manage to celebrate the inner marriage of the feminine and masculine aspects of Soul, on a personal level, we have come to a major achievement.
And, of course, we must never forget that the World has a Soul: Anima Mundi.

When Sun and Moon are in harmony (on both personal & worldly levels) is when we are At Home.
When they're not, is when we're really fucked.
And a lot on this planet, is.

Every one of the currently close on 70 billion Souls is a part of the Whole of It, and every one of Us has a part to play in It's all Coming Together.
This business is far too important for lower case letters.
Every one of Us carries a personal responsibility to the Healing.

A shrug of the shoulders; a "Whatever;" a "Not Me, Guv;" just will not do in a world where most of us have left some very negative trails-either in this life, or in past ones.
If we took Karma on board (I mean, really, on board), that when we "do the crime" so we "do the time," we'd be making the very big (and very necessary shift) to move this tired Old World into another gear.
Nobody said it would be easy; and anybody who said it would be, lied.

Old Moon Keeps on Making Her Mind Up

Full of feistiness in Aries,
And it shows.
She's going to get It right, this time,
And around two days to do it in.
Just got rid of Pisces, and She knows
She's still in, with a chance.
Just knows it!
Moon leads Herself a merry old dance,
And the rest of World with Her,
Tides let loose, pulling tight,
Surging through our deepest oceans.
In Cancer, She sorts debris.
In Scorpio, She burns.
In Aquarius, analyses, while World still turns.
Can't make Her mind up, in Gemini,
Argues in the Lion and the Bull.
In Libra, She's the diplomat.
In Virgo, seeks a harvest:
Yearns for It.
In Capricorn, is what She wants.
Sagittarius begs to differ:
It's what She needs: experience.
Moon's a Mirror held up to our Selves.

The Women Who Have Lost Their Voices

The women have lost their voices,
Not their true voices, rich mezzo sopranos, filled to their brims with music,
But the sorry, sorry voices
That come out so sad, because they were found wanting.
I cannot bear those notes that my own voice echoes
(that my own voice echoes)
When, in my head I hear you say:
I don't love you
(I don't love you)
So, how can I endure this choir of despair
Singing, in wretched contralto.
I never thought I would sing the notes
Of sorry, sorry voices.
While the basso profundo's sing they do not care/
Fuck you not caring, you destroyer's of the women's voices.
Fuck you men who make women so unhappy,
So that their voices are so sad.
The Wheel of Fortune turns, of course,
Each of you will become a woman
And then you will know.

One More Heavenly Light

When Sun did a bunk, as some Sun's do,
Moon was left, abandoned,
Fallen into Rue.
Not to put too fine a point on it,
Was left, holding the baby.
"Not Us, anymore," she sighed. "Just Me."
"Hang on," said the Child. "There's Me and You.
Everything's a Point of View."
Just one day old and, already in The Game.
"Moon's my Mother. Sun's my Dad.
Best beginning I've had.
So, another Myth began.
Moon called him "Man,"
And tried hard to be kinder.

When Peter Skellern Sings, He Makes me Cry

He does: it's the key he sings in,
Minor notes, and that brass band.
And that pause, a space, where I take a breath,
Remembering where we were;
When something needed music.
What's left is crying out for a song
Telling the whys, and wherefores,
And filling the gaps.
So, keeping still and waiting,
Tears begin to fall,
When Peter Skellern sings,

Moon's Feeling Feisty

"Could have told you," says Moon,
Handing down a handkerchief,
"I keep a stock of them,
For such as you weepers and wailers.
Bastards, all of them.
Why waste your tears?"
She's feisty: in the middle of Aquarius.
(So, why the fuck am I still stuck in Cancer?)
Giving me One of Her Looks, She continues.
"Look to your Nodes, Girl.
"You don't have to go out the way you came in.
You know the score.
Maiden, Mother Crone: you've been there
That swinging door's due to fall of its hinges, some day soon.
Here blow on this.
Remember you saw it coming, and didn't duck.
Some would.
Eat the pomegranate seeds and laugh.

Moon Says

Moon says, staring at me with one sad eye
And melancholy:
"Don't even think I can't see further,
With this one,
Than most can with more.
What are you for, exactly?"
She's in Pisces tonight.
Had one too many of just about everything.
Just about everything.
World, and me: what are we for?
The one eye wells with the pain of it,
And all her silver used up.

Oh, Happy Moon

I want to write a really Happy Poem about Moon,
When She's Off the Hook,
Swinging.
So, I will.
See.
She's dancing,
In Her own Light.

Her own Light, no Moonshine,
None borrowed from Sun.
She's worked out Her Time,
And is happy it's done.

No Cares, to speak of.
No axe to grind.
She's all out of Misery,
For Love has been kind.

All's come together,
And The World is at Peace.
Starlight, and Moonlight, and Earthlight all glow.
The Shadow is known.
She takes up her pen, dips deep in old tears,
The contract's been signed.
Now, She's up for the Book.
Sun will have His day, eventually.

Actually, says Moon

Actually, says Moon,
Being more communicative, when She's in Gemini,
I'm rather scared of flying.
Something to do with childhood.
My childhood.
(Giving Earth one of her looks)
You think You've got Issues!
Being torn from the Mother's womb, as I was,
(Said darkly, with innuendo)
Left a deep wound.
Who lights up my Dark Night
When I need some body?
Actually, says Earth, being in Taurus
And (mostly) practical
You think You've got problems.
This one Big Happy Family Thing is a misnomer.
Mine absolutely bugger up my Days.

Things Change

"Things change," says Moon.
And don't we know it?
Time and Again, we go through the Mill,
Being ground down to our grist.
Swings and Roundabouts.
Time to cut loose."
She laughs, daringly.
She's engaging in banter, being in one of Her lighter days.
I note, in my diary, that She's in Sagittarius.
"How about Las Vegas?"
Ply your chances: be the gambler:
Toss the coin.
"You'll never know unless you try.
Getting Ideas above your Station is
Just the Beginning
Of the Road,
To becoming a goddess."
She says.

You mustn't Fuck a Fairy
(A sad tale)

Oh, you mustn't fuck a fairy, else her s-elves will fight,
You really mustn't take her to the woods,
Unmake her, switch off her lights.
Oh no.
You shouldn't fuck a fairy.
Make her nights, and days, so bleak
You ought not to have done it, to entrap her,
So she lost the will to love, and speak.
That kind of thing, when you've stuffed her
Is, always, paid back, across the sands of time.
It's a crime.

Oh yes: it will come back to haunt you,
Stamping, as you did, on her wings.
When you fucked her up, fading her colours,
Making that final sting.
Her very s-elves were affronted,
And they'll unmask you,
And, with their quills, write on your dossier: "Karma,"
They will not be denied.

Your name's been writ, friend
(Or shall we call you foe?)
As the candle's burning low,
For, even as we speak, and in that leafy glen,
The only question's not where, but when.

Fish Wives

Where do they come from, these shrieking fish wives,
Hair dyed in rainbow colours,
Effing and blinding, like drunken gulls,
Lost souls who'd tear off your wipers, start a fight,
Take that smile off your face, as soon as look at you,
With their "Who are you looking at?" eyes.
Oh, those dead, flat-fish eyes;
Soused as herrings; kippered.
Oh, you Lost Souls., who never heard the music.
I'd magic you into mermaids, if I could,
All in a row,
Singing through the whole octave.

A Postcard

It's September: I'm in Dulwich.
There are foxes in the wood.
Shadows cast by Ziggy's fencing are lengthening.
Am I being understood?
London weather is fine, and settled.
A slug is on the lawn.
Had a restless night, as usual;
Always grow another skin, at dawn.
The slug is brown.
I'm listening to an operatic aria: Pavarotti's so sublime.
Carmen's found another lover.
Am I running out of time?
Seven buses are leaving Kuwait, heading for Bagdhad.
I'd thought of going down to Dover,
But the memories are too sad.
It's September: the wine is good.
Oh, I have worked, and I have lingered.
I've indulged my every whim.
Had my moments; smelled the blossoms
The sky's delightful: the wine is red.
How can it be that you are dead?
(Dover memories weren't that bad.
I try, so hard, not to be sad.)
Now, I say the things I never said,
And writing postcards in my head.
If I sang them, they'd be love songs.
If I wept, they'd be a dirge.
I'm just not sure how I can send them.
Can I use a power surge?
It's all guess work, where your sphere is:
Fire, Water, Earth, or Air?

My heart sends signals, loud and clear.
Life's the stuff that dreams are made on.
The food is good: wish you were here.

In 1986, in collaboration with the Head of Music at the School where we were teaching, I wrote a play , called "Making Sense." Then, I noted that the World's population was 4,000,755 million. On the script's introductory page, I had written:

"Whatever is "we" is surrounded by boned and flesh. Shakespeare called it "this goodly frame of aether."
It contains the people we love, and those we fear; and whatever is "we" looks out from, defends, and creates our world out of it. How is it, from shadings of difference, that we instantly recognise those whom we already "know"-and might love; and those whom we already know-and will choose to not love?
It is impossible to touch everyone in one life but our whole range of relationships with others, from mere recognition to a degree of sharing is expressed by how much we can open our eyes and really see."

At the end of each of the four nights in production, we had a balloon shower and the cast (actually numbering one tenth of the school population) all sang this final song.

"If we all got together,
Just think what we might do,
With the power of what is Me;
And the power of what is You.
If we all merged and mingled,
To light up all the World,
There's power in the Universe,
To do what we can do."

When I look back at that time, and who I am now, it's like looking at a distant relation. I am not the woman I was.
Every one of those I have met (whether in "good" or "bad" circumstances) have helped to make me what I am now.

When I first met the man who was to become my husband (this time around) and the father of my two sons, I found myself looking at a past life scenario. I was seventeen years old, and it was very confusing.

After the jerky images of this grey and black silent movie came to an end, I heard a voice which said:

"Well, you have a choice here. You can either leave right now, having made your apologies; or you can stay. The first option means you can have pretty much what you've dreamed about, in the way of material things. The second option means that while you won't have what most people would call "happiness" you'll learn a lot and you'll become a better person."

Actually, I can't recall making that decision. I think it was already made, and this, the reminder.
As to "better," I'll have to wait until I get back, for an answer.
As we all do.
And I'm, still, trying to make sense of it all.

About the Author

"My mother's name was given to me, backwards, which probably explains a lot. They were not a happy couple, and I've had a lot of unravelling to do," says Audrey.

"In attempting to look at Life from many different sides, and aspects of Love, every experience has brought something to light. From farming, to innkeeping, to teaching, to being drawn to healing, reading the Tarot cards, Astrology and Numerology, there has been a pattern. My hope is, it is in line with the web woven by the Fates & my Self, and that I've done more unravelling than ravelling."